PROMISED LAND

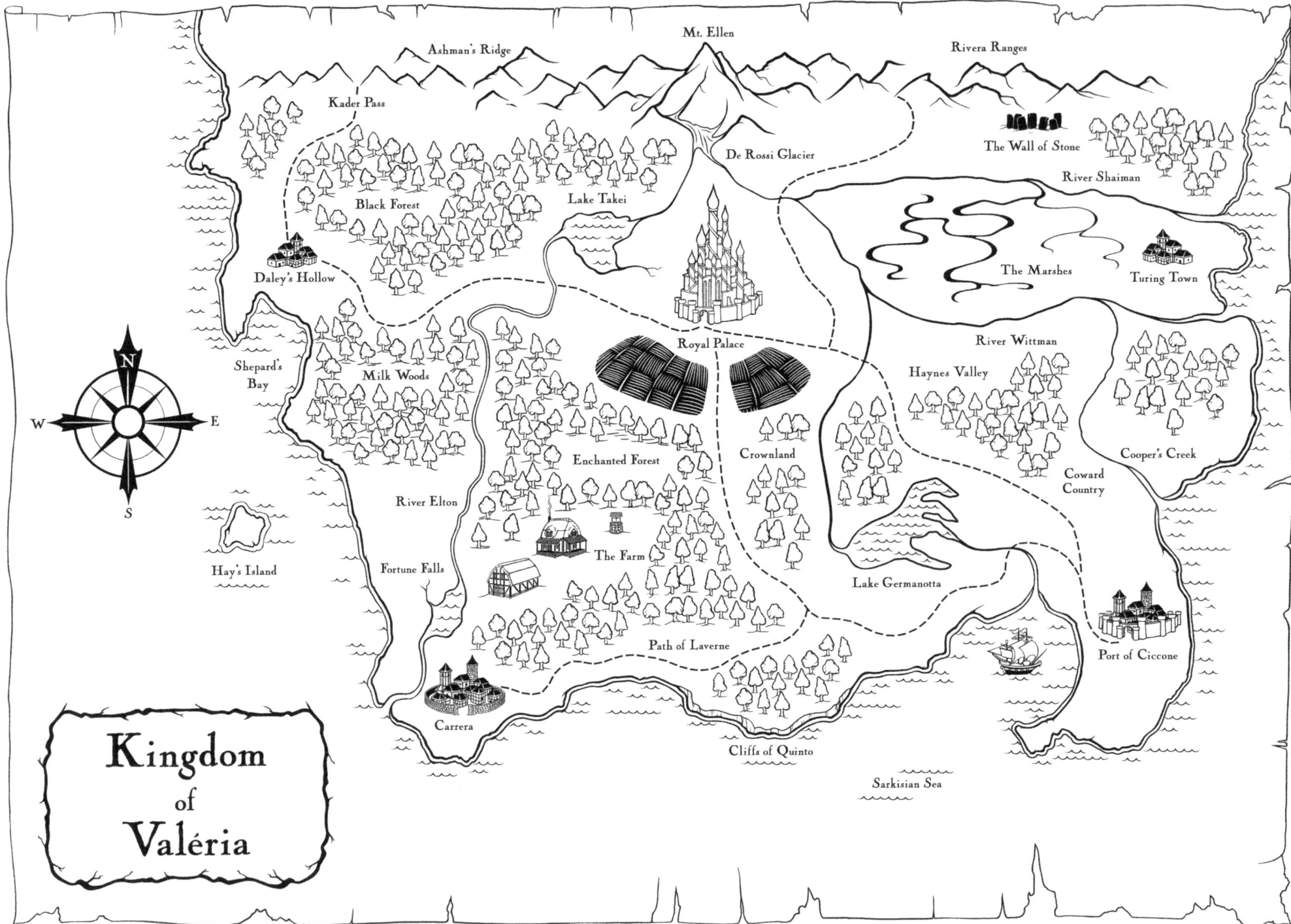

Ashman's Ridge

Mt. Ellen

Rivera Ranges

Kader Pass

De Rossi Glacier

The Wall of Stone

River Shaiman

Black Forest

Lake Takei

Daley's Hollow

The Marshes

Turing Town

Shepard's Bay

Royal Palace

River Wittman

Milk Woods

Haynes Valley

Enchanted Forest

Crownland

Cooper's Creek

River Elton

Coward Country

Hay's Island

The Farm

Lake Germanotta

Fortune Falls

Path of Laverne

Port of Ciccone

Carrera

Cliffs of Quinto

Sarkisian Sea

N
W   E
S

Kingdom
of
Valéria

PROMISED LAND

Illustrated by

Christine Luiten & Bo Moore

Based on the book written by

Adam Reynolds & Chaz Harris

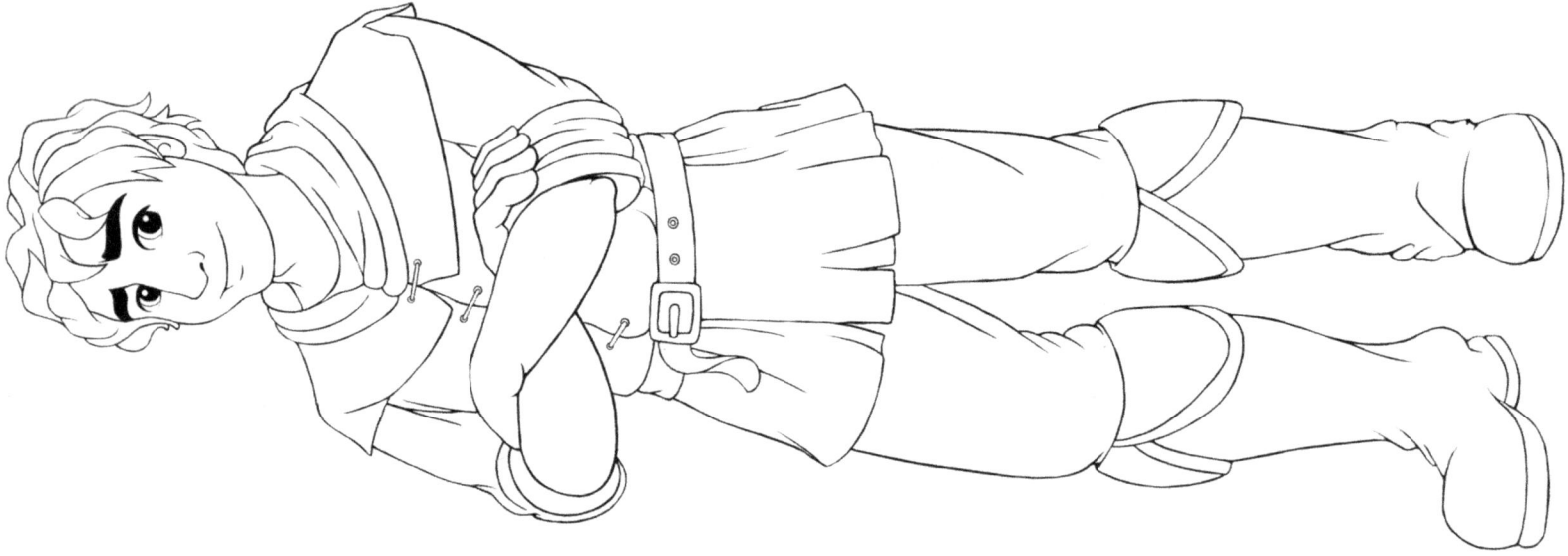

JACK

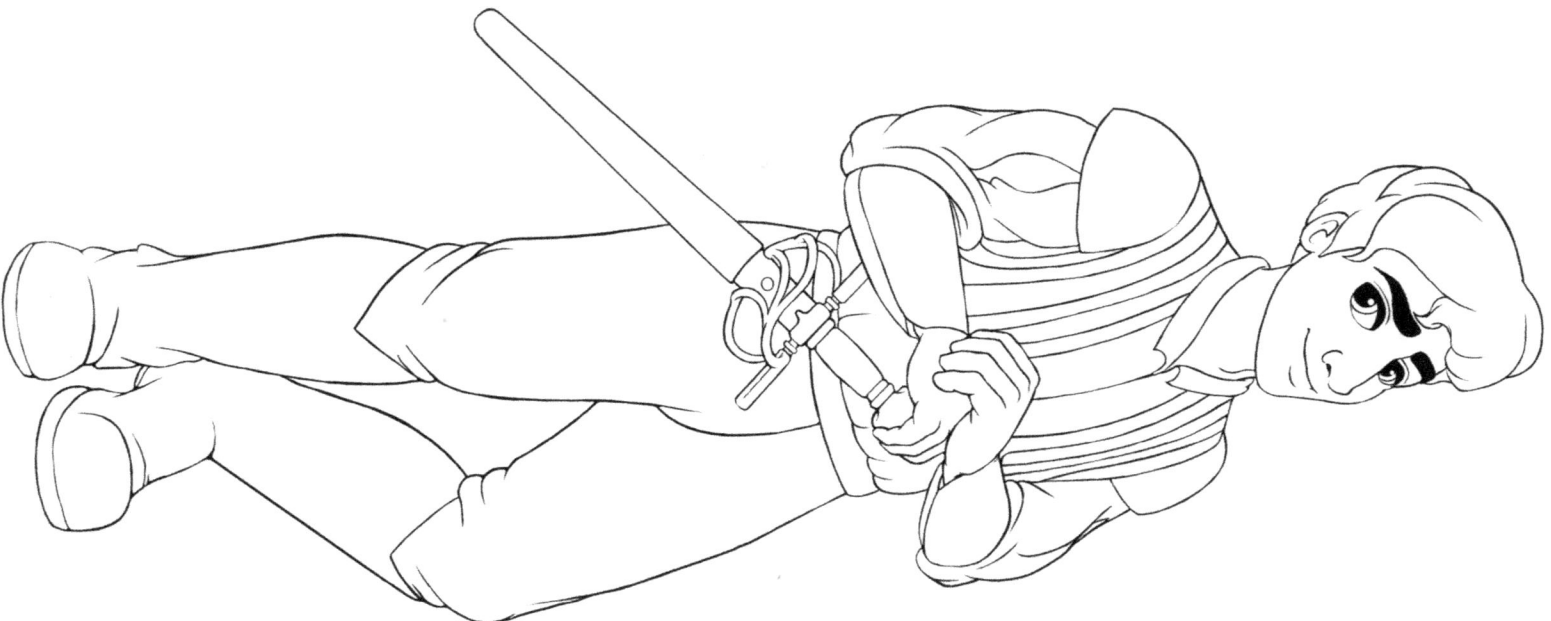

LEO

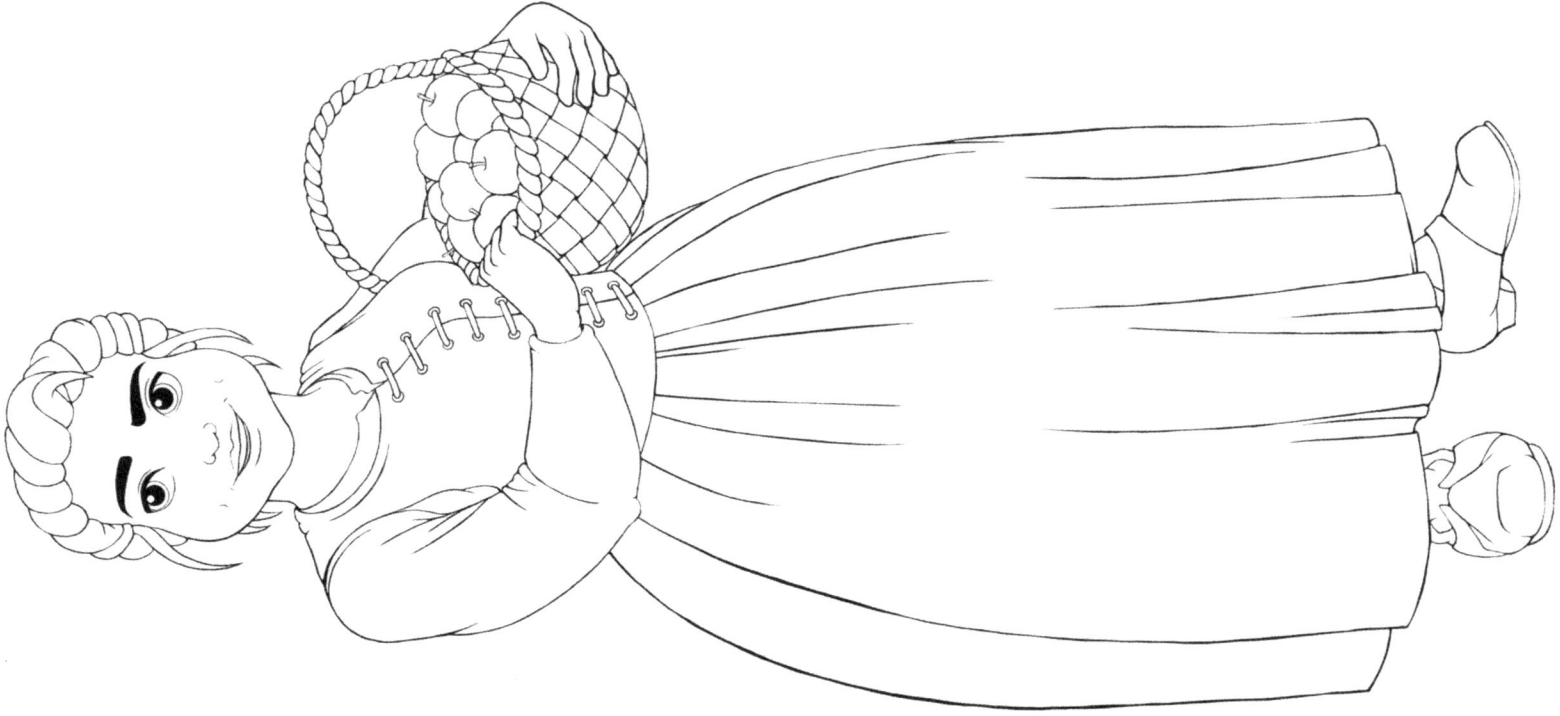

CAROL

Milo

QUEEN ELENA

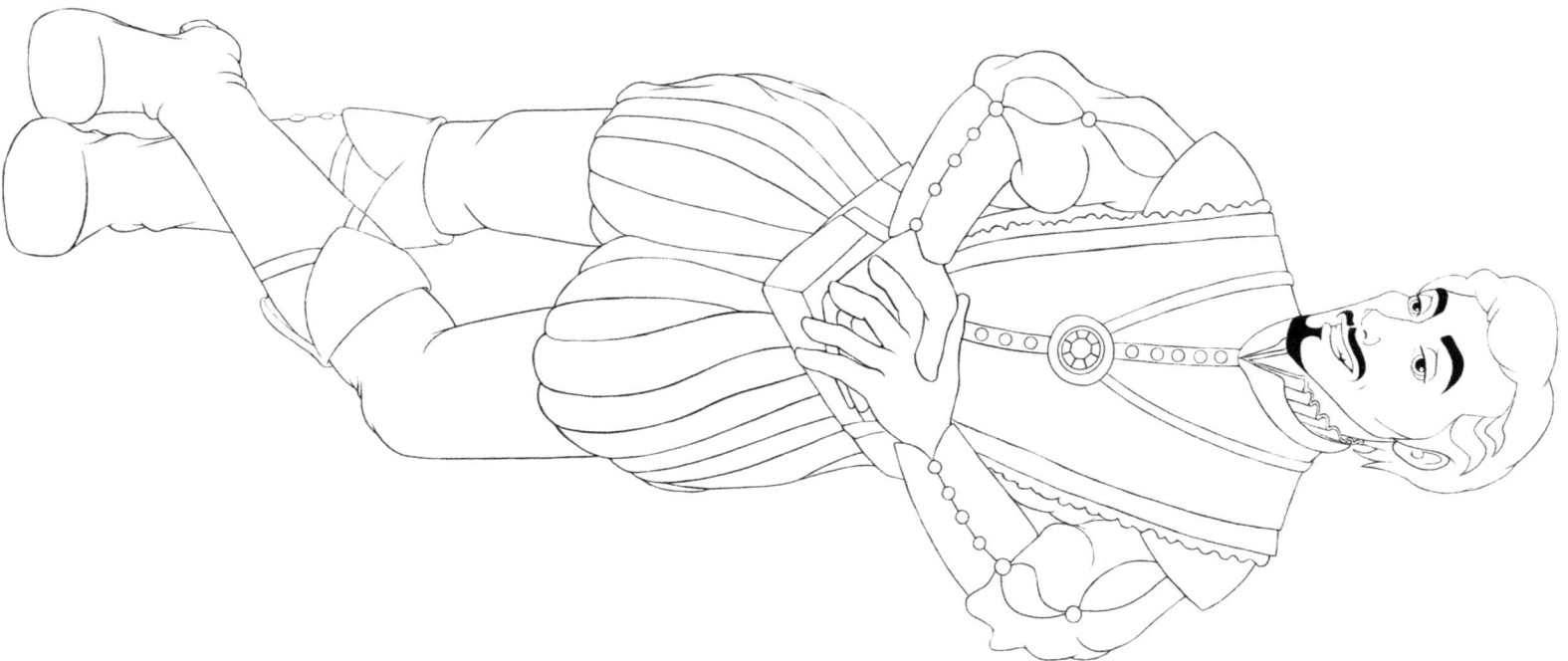

GIDEON

ISBN 978-0-473-39944-3

A catalogue record for this book is available from the National Library of New Zealand

Copyright © 2017 Promised Land Entertainment Ltd

www.promisedland-book.com

The End

The Legend of Eve